LOVE AN

2015 Re



# LOVE AND WAR

BY

**NADJA,**

*Author of 'The Evergreen.'*

LONDON

ARTHUR L. HUMPHREYS

187 PICCADILLY, W.

1915

**Reprinted in 2015 as a centenary reissue**

POSH UP NORTH Publishing

**www.poshupnorth.com**

**ISBN 978-1-909643-03-1**

**Re-edited by Paul Breeze**

***Note: a new foreword and biogrpahy by World War One researcher Lucy London has been added to the content of the original edition - as have new back pages.***

2015 Reprint

*Nadja (left) in Cannes with her mother in 1914*

Hommage de l'Auteur!

Nadja

.1915.

# CONTENTS

FOREWORD TO THE 2015 REPRINT BY LUCY LONDON 4
BRIEF BIOGRAPHY OF NADJA MALACRIDA 5

LOVE AND WAR - PART 1 – POEMS OF LOVE

INTRODUCTION........................................... 8
THE DREAM........................................ 8
MY GARDEN........................................ 9
LOVE'S FRIENDSHIP................................ 9
IN JUNE ........................................... 10
DESPAIR ........................................... 10
TO A SUNSET ...................................... 11
A RHAPSODY ...................................... 12
LOVE IN ABSENCE ................................ 13
LUCUBRATION ..................................... 13
AUTUMN ............................................ 14

LOVE AND WAR - PART 11 – POEMS OF WAR

INTRODUCTION....................................... 16
SEPTEMBER ......................................... 16
REGRET ............................................. 16
A FAREWELL ....................................... 17
TO A SOLDIER ..................................... 17
A SOLDIER'S PRAYER ............................ 18
A WOMAN OF ENGLAND ......................... 18
THE HARVEST ..................................... 19
THE EMPIRE TO HER FALLEN SONS ............... 20
REDEMPTION ....................................... 21
REQUIESCAT ....................................... 22

*Lucy London at her exhibition in Nelson, Lancashire in 2013*

## FOREWORD to the 2015 Reprint
## By Lucy London

I first found out about Nadja early on in my research, following publication of a letter I wrote to 'The Times' newspaper about Female Poets of the First World War.

I was contacted by Professor Brian Murdoch, Emeritus Professor of Literature and Languages at Stirling University, and we began exchanging correspondence.

Professor Murdoch had written an article about some of the female poets of the First World War including Nadja and was kind enough to send me a copy of his article, together with some examples of her work. The more I found out about Nadja, the more I admired her.

During the First World War, she had several volumes of poetry published and sold them in aid of St. Dunstan's, the home for military personnel blinded during the conflict that opened in 1915, and in aid of The Star and Garter Home that cared for wounded military personnel. The Star and Garter Home was opened in Richmond in 1916.

Both charities are still in existence today, though St. Dunstan's is now called Blind Veterans UK. You can find out more on their websites -

**https://www.blindveterans.org.uk/ and http://starandgarter.org/**

You can find out more about my other First World War projects by looking at these websites:

**www.femalewarpoets.blogspot.co.uk**
**www.inspirationalwomenofww1.blogspot.co.uk**
**www.fascinatingfactsofww1.blogspot.co.uk**
**www.forgottenpoetsofww1.blogspot.co.uk**

*Nadja in 1929*
*portrait by Lafayette*

# NADJA MALACRIDA

**(1895 – 1934)**
**POET, WRITER & BROADCASTER**

**A Brief Biography by Lucy London**

"Nadja" was the pen-name of Louisa Nadia Green, born in Hampstead in 1895, daughter of Mr and Mrs Charles Green and niece of Lord Cowdray, at whose home "Paddockhurst" in Sussex Nadja was raised.

By all accounts, she was an accomplished athlete and also obtained her pilot's licence as well as learning to speak French fluently. Nadja's first collection of poems (Evergreen) was published when she was fourteen years old and contained poems written when she was eight years old.

During the First World War, Nadja published three volumes of poetry - "Love and War" an anthology of poems which was published in 1915, "For Empire and other poems" published in 1916 (Arthur L. Humphreys) and "The Full Heart", published in 1919. All of these anthologies were sold in aid of St. Dunstan's Home for Blind Soldiers and The Star and Garter Home for Disabled Soldiers in Richmond.

On 6th December 1922 at St. Bartholomew the Great church in London, Nadja married Marchese Piero (Peter) Malacrida de Saint-August, an Italian Marquis.

They had met by chance on Alexandra Rose Day in 1921 at The Ritz in London where Nadja had been selling roses. Peter, who was a 'Northcliffe journalist', had just had a series of articles published in "The Daily Mail" and "The Evening News" about the German attitude to the war dead.

The couple were very much part of the London social scene in the 1920s and 1930s, and were seen at all the big society functions and parties. All of which was reported hungrily by the newspapers of the day. In the early 1920s, Nadja and Peter wrote a couple of novels called "Life Begins Here" and Footprints On The Sand" which were thinly disguised accounts of the London society scene.

Nadja was very much a celebrity of her time and appeared on early BBC Television broadcasts. She was regularly heard on BBC radio where she read out well known pieces of poetry. On the social circuit she was founder member of "The Happy Club" and also introduced the idea of 'causerie recital' musical evenings to London society.

Piero – or "Peter" - had studied engineering at Leeds University and was an interior designer, working on many prominent projects in London in the 1920s and 1930s. As such, the photogenic Nadja was often quoted in the newspapers of the day on matters of design and taste. She was even used as the face of "Vim" cleaner in a national newspaper advertising campaign.

In 1932, one of her plays – "The Cheque-Mate", which she wrote under the pseudonym "Lewis Hope" - had a short run at the Kingsway Theatre in London (25th May to 4th June 1932). The play starred actress Rosalind Fuller – who was big star of radio drama and cinema in those days - and attracted reviews in The Times and The Spectator.

The Malacridas were friends of Cecil Roberts the author who lent them his country cottage "Pilgrim Cottage" near Henley on Thames while he was away on a Greek cruise. On 3rd October 1934, Nadja was driving back to London when her car left the road and plunged down a 40 foot embankment. She was killed instantly

At the inquest, the Coroner was told that it was Najda's own car and she was a very experienced and competent driver. She had driven a car for 20 years, had previously driven at Brooklands motor racing circuit and even had a pilots licence.

Nadja was buried in Fairmile Cemetery in Henley-on-Thames, Oxfordshire.

*Nadja with Peter at Hanworth Aerodrome in 1932*

# PART I.

# POEMS OF LOVE.

## Introduction.

I SING of Springtime and the notes of songsters,
Of feathered breasts so full of joy and life,
Of happiness and sunshine, all abounding
Within a world where suffering is rife.
I praise sweet Nature and her lovely children,
Her gifts to Man in earth and Heav'n above:
I praise the Power that once created Nations,
And, praising Him, my heart is praising Love.

## The Dream.

I DREAMT we were together, and once more
I heard thy voice stirring my heart. Thine eyes
Gazed into mine, and all thy love I saw
In their blue depths. A thousand harmonies
Thrilled in our souls and yet the Tunes were One
In perfect Unison. Thy hand in mine
We watched the shadows of a Night begun
Veil all the sky with mystery divine.
Our hearts were full and still the words were few
That passed between us as we went our way.
A murmured vow to cherish and be true . . . .
The Night wore on, the darkness turned to Day
And on mine eyes the golden sunshine streamed.
Thy Face had vanished—thus it was I dreamed.

2015 Reprint

## My Garden.

WITHIN my garden side by side
Grow wondrous roses fair,
Their perfumes on the breezes glide
And linger everywhere.

Within the garden of my heart
A single flower grows free,
And as the roses scent impart
It breathes of Love for thee!

## Love's Friendship.

A TRUST implicit and a Love most pure,
A Patience noble and a Courage fine,
A Faith that will Eternity endure;
A Hope in God—and Mystery Divine.

A Prayer undaunted by the clouds of Life
And which the waves of Death may never break:
A Truth unfaltering on the breath of Strife—
And Honour, for our very friendship's sake.

## In June.

COME, gather roses, 'tis the time
  When Youth and Joy are springing
In one glad dance of madness sweet
With nimble, dainty, happy feet,
  And all the world is singing.

Come, wander in enchanted glades
  Where violets deep are growing,
And where the cuckoo sings his song
To all the happy feathered throng,
  And earth with peace is glowing.

Come, Youth and Love, whilst Spring is here
  And Life with Hope is thronging;
Chill Autumn comes too soon, and all
Is covered with her dread black pall,
  And naught is left but longing.

## Despair.

SOME months ago, when love first had its birth
  And when the pain I felt was wondrous new
And sweetly strange, I used to dream of you,
My eyes gazed ever upward, ne'er towards Earth.

And when the idle weeks had swept away
The mem'ries of our joy like fallen flowers,
I used to scan the path and count the hours,
That I might mark your coming, and be gay.

But now the months have passed apace and fled,
Leaving me hopeless, whilst mine eyes are bent
Wistful to earth, to seek which way you went;
No longer heavenwards, for Hope is dead.

# To a Sunset.

GOLD, gold all round, above me and about,
A wealth of colour and a feast of light;
A strain of music heralding the night,
A glimpse of Heaven ere the life dies out.

A million colours challenging the sea
To mirror all their charms upon its breast
Reign once supreme before the distant West
Dark'ning gives place to Night and bids them flee.

So brilliant are the shades that come and go,
Glittering strangely ere they fade and die,
The mountains rear their crests and glance below
To kiss the river as it hurries by.

So I look, musing, through the gathering mist,
And dream and hope as daylight fades away,
And Night creeps upward till it meets the Day—
The Stars above me whisper, 'They have kissed!'

# A Rhapsody.

A PEACEFUL night upon a golden stream,
When stars looked down to gaze upon their grace
That shone again thus doubly fair to see
Reflected in the river's hallowed face.

A night of nights, with Nature's softening hand
Stilling the breeze to murmur songs of love
Upon the reeds on yonder misty bank,
That glide away, then vanish up above.

We were not serious, but in jest our hearts
Thrilled to a mutual tune, and in thine eyes
I caught a glimpse of passing love and felt
My soul leap up to echo rhapsodies.

A look half tender, and a word half sighed
On lips just parted in a gentle smile;
And nothing to disturb the perfect peace
That swayed the world around us all the while.

Just such a night, now crowned with memories rare,
And radiant for those hours so soon to die,
An Interlude in life through which we passed
To smile without regret, and say 'Good-bye.'

## Love in Absence.

YET let me think you love me whilst the world
Sweeps by us in a seething, rushing band,
Like waves that by a mighty wind are curl'd
To Passion, ere they perish on the strand.

Let me but dream I love you, and the thought
Born in the night shall prosper all the day,
Till by my dreams the golden Truth is caught,
And thus I learn to love you far away.

## Lucubration.

I NEVER dreamt to love thee, dear, so much,
The thought of thee brought pleasure but not pain;
My pulse ne'er bounded at thine hallowed touch,
Nor beat my heart to welcome thee again
Until I knew that thou wast gone. Ah! then
Each hour grew heavy 'neath a load of tears,
Each cherished hope a deep resigned 'Amen,'
Torn from my heart amidst mine anguished fears.
Thus have I learnt to love thee when thy voice
No longer thrills the silence, and too late
I feel the fires that cause me to rejoice,
For thou art gone, and I can only wait.

## Autumn.

THE Summer-time which brought such happy love
Hath passed away, and sadness now creeps on
With Autumn: whilst the ever-falling leaves
Bid love and hope begone!
Cannot one ray of sunshine pierce the grey,
The thick, deep clouds of Autumn closing in?
Cannot one flower remain to cheer my life
And strike some hope within?
Unpitying Autumn lends a heedless ear
And sends strong winds to brush the leaves away;
The last red rose of Summer droops and dies,
Chilled by his kisses at the close of day.
So naught remains, and all have left me dead,
Dead to the world, and numbed by Autumn's breath,
Waiting for Spring to cheer and bring me hope,
Unless the Spring brings death.

# PART II.

# POEMS OF WAR.

## Introduction.

THEY found you in a barn, all three,
Deserted there in misery,
And all were crying bitterly:
You three.

They brought you home, two 'he's' one 'she,'
Called you Faith, Hope, and Charity,
And Charity remained with me,
You see!

She sits and plays beside my knee
And she is very fair to see,
So these few lines were penned by me
For Charity!

## September.

SEPTEMBER is a month for reaping tears
Where we have sown a smile,
The drifting leaves are like departed years
Forgotten in a while.

## Regret.

THINK not thou canst forget!
Those things in life that cast a gloom around
Are clearest in the heart and sooner found
When Memory spells Regret.

## A Farewell.

I HAVE the rippling of the mountain stream
Singing within my heart its joyful strain;
The shallow pools where Nature seems to dream
I carry with me, till I come again.

Scent-laden forests, where the pine-trees grow,
And heather moors ablaze with glorious light,
Sun-kissed at even when the breezes blow
That herald in another peaceful night.

All these I cherish as I go my way:
Sweet, precious memories that cannot die.
But evermore, beneath all else shall stay
The thought of unshed tears, and then 'Good-bye.'

## To a Soldier.

GO forth where Duty calls thee, soldier mine:
The hour has come, thy Country is at war,
Her honour is at stake and with it thine;
God speed thy footsteps till the fight be o'er,
And those, whose mission in this life must be
To wait and watch with tortured prayers of pain
Until the clouds disperse and shadows flee,
Shall welcome home their treasured ones again.

## A Soldier's Prayer.

GOD give me but the grace to stand
Patient and strong, with sword in hand,
To do my share for this dear land—
Perchance to die.

No earthly gifts I crave, dear Lord,
But that I may still bear this sword
Until the day when, Peace restored,
I lay it by.

## A Woman of England.

SHE was a woman; all herself was fair:
A guardian angel, tender, sweet and kind,
She lived amongst us: never has there been
More blest a nature than which blossomed there.
Her words were counsel, all her thoughts were true;
Full piteous unto sorrow drear was she,
And never was there anguish, grief, or pain
But came to her, and, coming, comfort drew.
Thus dwells her vision in this heart of mine,
And so I saw her, loved, and knew her grace;
And still I pray that King of kings to make
In all His Love, her womanhood divine.

# The Harvest.

IT was September: all the fields were gold—
Gold with the Harvest and the setting sun,
The woods and dales lay peaceful to behold,
And all the work was done.

And on that night the Reaper from above
Gathered a Harvest that He knew was best;
And to Himself, in perfect peace and love,
He bore my friend to rest.

It was September: all the world was fair,
Radiant with sunshine 'neath a cloudless sky;
But all the fields of corn and wheat are bare,
The Harvest is laid by.

# The Empire to her Fallen Sons.

THOU gavest a gift to me so wondrous rare
That all the love and faith I had in thee
Could not repay a sacrifice so dear
As that thou madest for me.

The price was great. The gift, thy Life, thine all:
Thou couldst not offer more to prove thy Love,
Oh! son of mine, when fighting thou didst fall
That I might tower above.

Think not in thy last moments that this gift
Shall be forgotten with its awful price,
Or that the Future with its clouds shall drift
Over thy Sacrifice.

Thou gav'st thy Life that I in Peace might reign,
A proof supreme, untempered by regret,
Of thy great Love. It was not given in vain ....
Britain will not forget.

# Redemption.

LISTEN! the sound is as rumbling thunder,
Crashing and snapping and rending the air;
All blindly pressing, some falling under,
Hurries the crowd seeking help anywhere.
Panic, confusion and terror are spreading,
Faces are blanched, eyes with horror are wide,
Some for the houses and shelter are heading,
Others are finding the broad country-side.
Women and children, the way scarcely heeding,
Fight for their lives through the turmoil and
crowd,
Stumbling and falling, to lie bruised and bleeding,
Beaten to death 'neath that vast moving shroud.
High in the heavens great flashes are glaring,
Houses are crumbling masses of stones,
Barns are alight and with hungry flames flaring;
Drowned are the echoes of heart-rending groans.

Only one thing that is not harmed and broken
Towers o'er the chaos of murder and loss;
But of Redemption assured 'tis the token,
The suffering figure of Christ on the Cross.
Tranquil, aloft amidst all that is shattered,
Emblem of Peace in this storm-laden hour
Bring to Thyself all those souls that are scattered—
God shall repay, for of Him is all Power.

# Requiescat.

WE sought for you amidst the ruined homes,
In many a churchyard and 'neath many a wall,
In lonely places when long shadows fall
Haunted by Death who restless creeps and roams,
Tired by his wand'rings through the misty air,
Amazed to find that he is everywhere.

We sought for you beneath the apple-trees
Laden with blossoms on that bright Spring morn,
And though our hearts with agony were torn,
Our lips praised God who sent the tender breeze
To murmur in our ears calm words of love
Flowing in mercy from His Throne above.

My Love, we found you when the light had fled
Within the shelter of a peaceful wood,
And there we knelt to touch the cross that stood
Marking the spot where rested your dear head;
And as we left you on our hearts there fell
A wondrous Peace that told us—'All is well.'

2015 Reprint

# More Great Books Available by Mail Order From The Same Publisher!

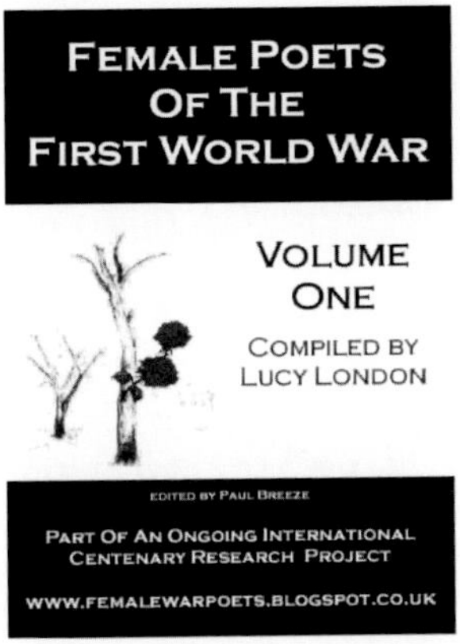


**FEMALE POETS – VOLUME 1**

This is so much more than "just" an anthology of poetry as Lucy sets out to uncover and celebrate the works of lesser known - or maybe forgotten - women who wrote during the First World War.

The are short biographies of the poets involved, photos and lots of other bits and pieces that will be of interest to anyone who wants to know more about that world-changing period of recent history.

Compiled by Lucy London / Edited by Paul Breeze
ISBN 978-1-909643-02-4
126 pages paperback perfect bound

**NO WOMAN'S LAND**

Included in this first volume are:
Doctors and Nurses, including Mabel Stobart, Flora Murray, Edith Cavell and Nellie Spindler
Female Fighters, such as Flora Sandes and Milunka Savic
Writers and diarists such as May Sinclair, Mildred Aldridge and Inez Milholland
Plus female spies, female pilots and whole lot more besides!

Compiled by Lucy London / Edited by Paul Breeze
ISBN 978-1-909643-07-9
128 pages paperback perfect bound

**GUNS & PENCILS**
**A Collection Of War Poetry**

By Lucy London
Published 2012

ISBN: 978-0-9539782-2-9
20 pages softback stapled
**Selling Price: £4.00**
UK inland postage & packing £1.50

Please enquire for other destinations

**PURPLE PATCHES**
**A Collection Of Poems, Songs And Short Stories From The Fountain Pen of Lucy London**

By Lucy London
Edited by Paul Breeze
Features sketches by Lucy London and several photographs
Published 2013
ISBN: 978-1-909643-00-0
42 pages paperback perfect bound

**Selling Price: £4.00 plus p&p**

**BLACKPOOL TO BOND STREET!**
**The fascinating story of Amy Blackburn - pioneer of the makeover**

By Joan Shaw

Published 2007
ISBN: 978-0-9539782-5-0
60 pages softback perfect bound
photographs throughout

**Selling Price: £6.00**

**See more great books at www.poshupnorth.com**